NAVY SEALs

NAVY
SEALs

CHRIS MCNAB

amber
BOOKS

Published by
Amber Books Ltd
74–77 White Lion Street
London
N1 9PF
United Kingdom
www.amberbooks.co.uk
Appstore: itunes.com/apps/amberbooksltd
Facebook: www.facebook.com/amberbooks
Twitter: @amberbooks

ISBN: 978-1-78274-477-1

Project Editor: Sarah Uttridge
Designer: Trudi Webb
Picture Research: Terry Forshaw

Printed in China

PICTURE CREDITS:

Alamy: 16/17 (Richard Ellis), 54/55 (Everett Collection)

Cody Images: 12-15 all

Getty Images: 55 (David Turnley), 59 (Aamir Qureshi)

US Air Force: 58/59

US Army: 40, 40/41

US Department of Defense: 7, 10/11, 52, 56/57

US Marines: 31

US Navy: 4, 8/9, 9, 18, 20/21, 21, 25, 26, 26/27, 28/29, 29, 30/31, 32-39 all, 46/47,
   48/49, 49, 50/51, 57, 60, 60/61

US Navy SEALs: 2/3, 6/7, 16, 18/19, 22/23, 42-45 all, 46, 50, 52/53, 63

CONTENTS

INTRODUCTION

You have to be tough and strong to make it into the U.S. Navy SEALs.

WHAT DOES "SEAL" MEAN?

The word "SEAL" stands for "SEa, Air, and Land." The United States Navy SEALs fight in many places. They fight at sea from boats and also work as divers. They fight in the air from helicopters and airplanes, parachuting from heights. They fight on the land as expert warriors.

NAVY WARRIORS

The SEALs are actually part of the U.S. Navy, not the U.S. Army. This does not mean that the SEALs spend all their time on ships. Instead, they perform every different type of mission, from rescuing hostages to raiding enemy bases.

SPECIAL FORCES

The SEALs are part of Special Operations Forces soldiers. This means that they perform difficult or dangerous missions that often can't be performed by typical soldiers. They have special training for these missions in enemy territory.

BECOMING A SEAL

To become a SEAL, you have to pass the world's hardest military training.

TEAM EFFORT

Many people don't succeed in passing the training program to become a U.S. Navy SEAL. In fact, if 10 people try to become SEALs, about eight or nine will fail. The people who do pass are some of the very best warriors in the world.

WOMEN SEALs
Women can now apply to join the SEALs. Until 2015, only men were able to join the SEALs. Women have to pass the same training as the men.

NAVY CLASS

Each year, a class of men and women begin the U.S. Navy SEAL training program. They must be patient and pass each stage of training. It can take more than two years for SEALs to go from beginning their training to heading out on their first mission.

SMALL UNITS

SEALs usually train and fight in small groups, not in large units. The smallest group is the two-person "buddy" team.

SEAL HISTORY

The story of the SEALs began in World War II, a war that lasted from 1939 to 1945.

SCOUTS AND RAIDERS

In 1942, the U.S. Army and Navy created a special new force of soldiers. They were called "Scouts and Raiders." They were trained to make secret missions onto beaches where American invasion forces would later land. These soldiers performed some of the same kinds of missions as the modern U.S. Navy SEALs.

DEMOLITIONS

Three Scouts and Raiders units were created. They performed missions across the world. Another U.S. force was called the Naval Combat Demolition Teams. These men were responsible for blowing up enemy obstacles on beaches.

UDTs

In November 1943, the U.S. Marine Corps began forming Underwater Demolition Teams (UDTs) to work in the Pacific Ocean. The UDTs used diving equipment and boats to attack enemy positions on beaches that the military was invading. The SEALs were formed out of the UDTs.

DIVERS

The United States was one of the first nations to train soldiers in the skills of what we call "combat diving."

MAKING MAPS

A big role of the new units was to secretly study enemy beaches. They would then make maps of the beaches to help invasion forces land.

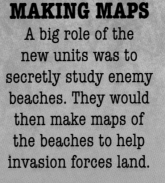

WWII OPERATIONS

During World War II, combat divers and UDTs worked on many dangerous missions.

ACROSS THE WORLD

During World War II the U.S. military had thousands of men trained in the skills of "amphibious warfare." Amphibious warfare means fighting from the water to the land. These men fought in places such as France, Africa, the islands of the Pacific Ocean, and China.

GUNBOATS

Units such as the UDTs would use boats heavily armed with machine guns. The boats would take divers close in to the enemy shorelines.

DIVING INTO ACTION

During World War II, the U.S. government had a secret organization called the Office of Strategic Services (OSS). In 1943, the OSS created a group of men called "Operational Swimmers." They were trained in combat diving, and they were very similar to today's U.S. Navy SEALs.

BLOWING UP

Units such as the UDTs were trained to blow up enemy buildings and obstacles. They would use large packs of explosives.

SEALs IN VIETNAM

The SEALs were formed in the 1960s by order of the president.

VIETNAM WAR

During the Vietnam War (1955 to 1975), the United States sent soldiers to help South Vietnam fight against invaders from North Vietnam.

THE SEALs ARE FORMED

In 1962, President John F. Kennedy gave permission to create SEAL Teams 1 and 2 during the Vietnam War. They were formed out of the UDTs. Their job was to fight enemy soldiers in the rivers and jungles, as well as along the coastlines of South Vietnam and North Vietnam.

RIVER RAIDS

The SEALs were trained to go deep into enemy territory in Vietnam. They would hide in the jungle and spot enemy bases. Then SEAL teams would use boats to sail up rivers and destroy the enemy bases with machine guns and explosives. The "Viet Cong" enemy was afraid of the SEALs, who attacked without warning.

HUNTING

The SEALs spent much of their time during the Vietnam War in the Mekong Delta. This area in South Vietnam has thousands of miles of rivers where enemy soldiers would hide.

LOSSES

From 1965 to 1972 a total of 49 U.S. Navy SEALs were killed in Vietnam. Lieutenant Melvin S. Dry was the last to die, in October 1972.

SEAL OPERATIONS 1973–91

After the Vietnam War, the SEALs continued to fight for their country.

GRENADA

In 1983, U.S. soldiers invaded the island of Grenada to restore its government. SEAL teams 4 (see left) and 6 provided "recon" (see page 17) of the invasion areas.

GULF WAR

In 1991, many SEALs fought in a large war, known as the Gulf War, against the country of Iraq. It had invaded the country of Kuwait. Like the two men seen here, the SEALs fought in Kuwait City, which had been captured by the enemy. The SEALs also attacked oil refineries held by Iraqi soldiers.

PANAMA MISSION

In December 1989, the SEALs helped in the U.S. invasion of Panama. They destroyed the boat and jet aircraft belonging to Panama's president, who had committed serious crimes. The mission was a success, although four SEALs were killed during the fighting.

RECON ROLES

"Recon" is a short version of the word "reconnaissance." It refers to the military's efforts to discover the enemy's location.

SEAL FACT

During the Gulf War, SEALs tricked Iraqi troops into thinking a U.S. invasion would take place where it didn't.

SEAL OPERATIONS 1991–PRESENT

SEALs continue to serve in the frontline of the U.S. military.

AFGHANISTAN

Since 2001, SEALs have fought many battles in the country of Afghanistan, fighting the enemy in the fields, villages, and mountains. Many have lost their lives, such as Lieutenant Michael P. Murphy (see left), who was killed in action in 2015.

HIGHEST MEDAL

Lieutenant Murphy was awarded the Medal of Honor as a tribute to his bravery. This is the United States' highest military medal.

IRAQ WAR

Beginning in 2003, the SEALs fought in another war against Iraq. In one battle, U.S. Air Force helicopters dropped the SEALs onto an important Iraqi dam. The SEALs captured and held the dam. During the mission, they worked alongside specially trained soldiers from Poland.

SEAL FACT

SEALs are often used to train the soldiers of other nations. The SEALs teach skills like shooting, handling explosives, and using radios.

COMBAT MISSIONS

The SEALs have to be ready for any operation around the world, at any time.

RESCUE MISSIONS

Some SEAL teams are trained in rescuing hostages. Hostages are people who have been taken prisoner by enemy forces. In April 2009, SEAL snipers killed three African pirates who were holding an American ship captain hostage.

COVERT OPS

The SEALs often take part in secret missions. The official name for these missions is "covert operations."

THE U.S. NAVY

The U.S. Navy sends its ships all around the world. SEAL teams are usually part of a Carrier Battle Group, like the one seen here. The Carrier Battle Group is a large group of ships. The most powerful warship in the group is an aircraft carrier.

The helicopters here are called HH-60H Seahawks. They are landing SEALs on the deck of a U.S. Navy ship.

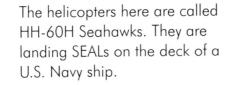

SEAL SNIPER

A sniper is trained to shoot the enemy with a rifle from a long distance. The SEALs often use snipers in rescue missions.

BRAVE PEOPLE

Being a SEAL is a dangerous job. On August 6, 2011, 17 SEALs died when their helicopter was shot down over Afghanistan. Many other American and Afghan soldiers were also killed in this incident. They were flying to help other American soldiers.

SEAL UNITS

The SEALs are part of a larger organization called the Naval Special Warfare Command (NSWC).

SEAL GROUPS

The SEALs are divided into Groups and Teams. There are four Naval Special Warfare Groups in total. Each group trains to fight and operate in different parts of the world. Group One and Group Two each have four SEAL teams.

SEAL TEAMS

There are a total of eight SEAL teams. Each team usually has about 300 people in it. Four of the teams are based in Coronado in California, and four of the teams are in Little Creek, Virginia. Below are some official badges of different teams.

SDVTs

Other NSWC units help the SEALs. Two SEAL Delivery Vehicle Teams (SDVTs) help move SEAL teams into position from special submarines. The submarines can take the SEALs silently up to enemy coastlines.

SMALL FORCE

There are only about 2,450 SEALs in the U.S. Navy. This might seem to be a lot, but the whole Navy has more than 300,000 people.

BOAT OPERATORS

The Navy has Special Warfare Combatant-Craft Crewmen (SWCC). Three Special Boat Teams (SBT) are part of the SWCC. These sailors are trained to take Special Operations Forces into action on small boats.

SEAL TEAMS

The SEALs are arranged into small teams that can be called instantly into action.

ORGANIZATION

Each SEAL team is commanded by a U.S. Navy officer known as a commander. The team is split into smaller units called "platoons." Each platoon has 16 people. When they perform missions, the platoon can be broken down into even smaller units. In fact, just two SEALs can work together as a single unit if necessary for the mission.

MOTTO

One of the mottoes of the U.S Navy SEALs is "The only easy day was yesterday." It means that a SEAL has to give maximum effort every day.

WORLDWIDE

SEALs can be sent anywhere in the world on missions. For this reason, they train in many different countries and situations.

8-MAN TEAM

Eight-man squads or four-man "fireteams" are the most usual sizes for SEAL units on a mission.

SEAL TEAM 6

"SEAL Team 6" is the short name for the least-known NSW force. It is actually called the U.S. Naval Special Warfare Development Group (NSWDG), or DEVGRU. This unit performs some of the most secret and dangerous missions around the world, so their faces have been hidden in the picture on the right.

RECRUITING

Every year more than 1,000 people try to join the SEALs.

WHO JOINS THE SEALs?

There are three types of people who join the SEALs. The first are people who are already serving in the U.S. Navy. The second type are people in other parts of the armed forces, such as the Army. The third group is made up of civilians (people who aren't in the armed forces) who want to go straight into the SEALs.

HOW TO START

To be a U.S. Navy SEAL, you must be a U.S. citizen. Then you have to see a person called a Naval recruiter. He or she will assess if you are able to join the SEALs and will arrange for you to have physical tests to see if you are fit enough. You also have to complete intelligence tests.

THE ASVAB
To enter SEAL training you must pass the Armed Services Vocational Aptitude Battery (ASVAB), which tests your thinking skills.

USS
ENTERPRISE
CVN 65

AGE RANGE

All people who join the SEALs are volunteers. They must be between 18 and 29 years old.

GETTING FIT

SEAL training is very hard and tests the recruits' strength and fitness to their limits.

PASSING THE PST

To enter SEAL training, you first have to pass a Physical Screening Test (PST). This has five parts. You must be able to swim 500 yards (460 meters) in at least 12 minutes and 30 seconds. You have to be able to do at least 50 sit-ups in two minutes, and 50 push-ups in two minutes. You have to be strong enough to do 10 pull-ups. Finally, you must run 1½ miles (2.4 kilometers) in at least 10 minutes 30 seconds. Remember, however, that these are the minimum requirements—the SEALs want to see you do much better than this.

During SEAL training the recruits will end up doing hundreds of push-ups every single day.

NO GAMING

SEAL trainers say that before you begin SEAL training, you should spend most of your time playing sports and doing fitness activities, not computer games.

INJURIES

One of the biggest reasons people fail SEAL training is because they injure themselves. SEAL training is hard on your body, particularly your ankles, knees, hips, and shoulders. It is important to do many strength and stretching exercises before training begins.

THE C-SORT

The SEALs need people with strong minds. Civilian recruits do a test called C-SORT. This computer exam shows if they have a tough personality.

THROUGH THE PAIN

The SEAL physical training is designed to push recruits to their limits. It reveals who will give up and who will keep going.

PREP SCHOOL

Preparatory Schools get the new recruits ready for the training ahead.

PREPARATORY SCHOOL

Once you have passed the PST and C-SORT, and before you start the main part of SEAL training, you have to go through Preparatory School. This period of training lasts for eight weeks. Its purpose is to make the recruits fit enough to go on to the next stage of the program. The tests that the recruit took as part of the PST are now made much more difficult. If recruits cannot pass these tests, then they cannot go on to become a U.S. Navy SEAL.

SWIMMING

In the Prep School swimming test, the recruit must eventually be able to swim 1094 yards (1,000 meters) while wearing "fins." These are paddle-like shoes that divers wear on their feet. The recruits have to swim this distance in 20 minutes or less.

LONG RUN

During the Prep phase, the recruits have to run four miles (6.4 kilometers) in 31 minutes or less. They wear training shoes and pants.

SWIM TIP

Practice swimming wearing fins. It will make your ankles stronger for real SEAL training.

SUPPORT

SEAL trainers do not want people to fail the training. For this reason, SEAL trainers and veterans are always on hand to provide advice and guidance to people trying to pass Prep School. However, during the Prep phase, trainers also want to see recruits take responsibility for their own success or failure.

TRAINING

The toughest part of the SEAL training is called Basic Underwater Demolition/SEAL, or BUD/S for short.

BUD/S TEST

A lot of people drop out of SEAL training. Many drop out during the Basic Conditioning phase of the BUD/S program.

BUD/S: FIRST PHASE

BUD/S lasts for six months in total. The main part of BUD/S has three phases. The first phase is called Basic Conditioning. This lasts for seven weeks and is held in Coronado, California. It focuses on hard physical training on the land and in the water. It includes a period called "Hell Week."

SECOND PHASE

The second phase of BUD/S also lasts seven weeks. During this time, the recruits are trained in combat diving.

D.O.R.
If recruits want to stop the training, they can drop out at any time. They become "Dropped on Request" (D.O.R.).

THIRD PHASE

The third phase of BUD/S lasts seven weeks, too. During this time, the recruits are trained in all the skills of land warfare. This means that they learn how to fight the enemy on the land. During this phase they gain experience in shooting guns.

HELL WEEK

"Hell Week" takes place during the fourth week of the main BUD/S training.

NO SLEEP

Hell Week actually lasts for five and a half days. During that time, recruits only sleep about four hours in total. The instructors put the recruits through constant, exhausting physical exercises, such as carrying telegraph poles.

BRAVING THE WAVES

In one Hell Week exercise, the recruits must take small inflatable boats through crashing waves. The waves will often flip the boat over.

RUN THE DISTANCE

During Hell Week the recruits will run more than 200 miles (322 kilometers). They will make the runs while wearing military uniform and carrying heavy military backpacks and weapons.

SURF TEST

Recruits are made to lie in the freezing waves flowing onto a beach. They get so cold that they shiver uncontrollably, but they are not allowed to get up.

POOL TRAINING

During "drownproofing," SEALs are made to bob up and down in a swimming pool with their wrists and ankles tied up.

COMBAT DIVING

The Combat Diving phase is the part of training that begins to turn recruits into SEALs

POOL TRAINING

The Combat Diving phase of BUD/S is designed to teach the recruits how to use diving gear with total confidence. Much of the training takes place inside a large swimming pool, where the recruits can be watched safely by the instructors.

NIGHT DIVING
SEALs must learn how to dive at night, a difficult skill since it is easy to get lost under water at night, especially in murky waters.

EMERGENCIES

Combat Diving teaches the recruits to deal with all sorts of emergencies under water. These can include what to do if you suddenly run out of oxygen. The recruits are also trained in how to rescue drowning people.

CONFIDENCE

In the Combat Diving phase, instructors pull away the recruits' air supply under water to test that they do not panic under pressure.

OPEN WATER

From the pool, the recruits will move on to swimming in open seas, coastal waters, and in rivers. They must learn how to use advanced diving equipment in these places.

CLASSROOM

The recruits will also spend a lot of time in the classroom. There they will find out all about the science and medical issues of diving.

SEAL QUALIFICATION TRAINING

After Combat Diving, the SEAL recruits learn how to fight like soldiers during Land Warfare and SEAL Qualification Training (SQT).

LAND WARFARE

The Land Warfare phase teaches the recruits to fight as a team and on their own. They learn how to handle guns and how to find their way in the wilderness. They will also learn about tactics. One of the special skills during this phase is how to slide down a rope from a helicopter. This is called "fast-roping."

SEAL TRIDENT

If recruits pass SQT, they become official U.S. Navy SEALs. They are given the SEAL trident badge to wear on their uniform.

SQT

If the recruits pass the Land Warfare phase, they go on to SEAL Qualification Training. This training lasts for 26 weeks. It teaches the recruits the advanced skills that will make them SEALs. These skills include handling explosives, surviving being held a prisoner, and performing first aid during combat.

FIRST AID

SEALs are trained to treat injuries on the battlefield. This is a vital skill since SEALs often go on missions where doctors are not there to help.

PARACHUTING

SQT includes training in how to make parachute jumps. The recruits have to become experts in all types of jumps, such as free fall.

FREE FALL

In free fall parachute jumps, SEALs drop a long way before opening their parachute.

SPECIAL PATROL INSERTION/ EXTRACTION (SPIE) SYSTEM

The U.S. Navy SEALs use the SPIE system to move quickly by helicopter.

BEHIND ENEMY LINES

SEALs often use helicopters to take them behind enemy lines—this is called "insertion." Helicopters will also be used to pick them up when they need to get out—this is called "extraction." Sometimes the helicopters are not able to land because the area is too dangerous for them. This is why the SPIE system was developed and is used by the SEALs.

INFILTRATION

"Infiltration" is crucial to the SEALs. It means the ability to move into an enemy area without being detected.

PICK-UP SYSTEM

In the SPIE system, a special rope is attached to the bottom of a helicopter. The rope is dropped down to the SEALs watching below. Each SEAL is wearing a harness, and they clip the harness onto the dangling rope.

LIFT OFF

Once the SEALs are safely clipped onto the rope, the helicopter can then lift away. As the helicopter rises, they are hoisted into the air on the rope. The helicopter pilot flies away and takes the SEALs to a landing zone where he or she can lower them down safely. Obviously, the pilot must watch out for dangerous obstacles below the helicopter on the way.

RESCUE
The SPIE system can also be used by the SEAL team to rescue people from water and other dangerous locations.

EQUIPMENT

The SEALs have some of the best military equipment in the world.

WEAPONS

SEALs must be experts in handling all sorts of firearms. Each soldier has a rifle and a pistol. This SEAL is using a powerful rifle known as an FN SCAR. Using the telescopic sight he will be able to hit targets hundreds of yards (meters) away.

Ammunition pouches

Lightweight backpack and drinking pouch

SiG P226 pistol

Karabiner clip for climbing

SPECIAL CLOTHING

In freezing environments, the SEALs wear arctic clothing that protects them from the cold, wet, and windy conditions. Goggles protect their eyes from the glare of the sun off the snow. These uniforms are camouflage white. SEALs will also camouflage their weapons with white strips of cloth or paint.

HEAVY LOADS

During training and operations, a SEAL might have to carry more than 100 pounds (45 kilograms) of equipment.

BODY ARMOR

SEALs often wear body armor on missions. The armor is strong enough to stop a rifle bullet and bomb splinters.

BURST COMMS

Some SEAL radios use "burst communications." They can record a message and broadcast it in a fraction of a second.

DIVING GEAR

SEAL diving gear is designed with military operations in mind.

SCUBA APPARATUS

For basic diving, SEALs wear an "open-circuit" SCUBA breathing apparatus. This uses an air tank worn on the back. When the SEAL breathes out, air bubbles are pushed into the water.

DPV SYSTEMS

Rather than swimming, SEALs can use Diver Propulsion Vehicles (DPVs), small machines that pull the diver through the water.

REBREATHING SYSTEM

The problem with standard SCUBA gear is that the bubbles can give away a SEAL's position when they burst on the surface. For this reason, SEALs also train with "rebreathers." These diving systems do not release bubbles. Instead, they reuse the air that the diver breathes out.

NAVIGATION BOARDS

To find their way in dark or murky water, the SEALs carry "navigation boards." These pieces of equipment carry at least a compass, dive watch, and a depth gauge. Some of the navigation boards even have a fitting for a combat knife.

WETSUITS

SEAL wetsuits have a special fitting for a radio earpiece in the hood. This enables the diver to listen to radio messages while under water.

LAND VEHICLES

Some of the SEALs' most exciting pieces of gear are their combat vehicles.

HUMVEE

Like the rest of the U.S. military, the SEALs use the "Humvee" vehicle. The Humvee is tough and powerful. It can be fitted with different weapons. This SEAL Humvee has a Browning M2HB machine gun on top.

DPV DRIVING

The Desert Patrol Vehicle (DPV) is a dune buggy used to move quickly over rough land. It can be fitted with machine guns and antitank missile launchers.

DPVs IN ACTION

DPVs like the ones seen here were used in Kuwait and Iraq in 1991.

ALSV

As well as the DPVs, the SEALs use the Chenowth Advanced Light Strike Vehicle (ALSV). These vehicles are light enough to be carried inside a large helicopter. SEALs have used them in wars in Iraq and Afghanistan since 2011.

DRIVER SKILLS

SEALs are trained in combat driving skills. They must learn how to drive across rough terrain without tipping the vehicles over.

HUMVEE FACT

The Humvee has a maximum speed on the road of 70 miles (113 km) per hour. On rough terrain, its speed is 55 miles (88 km) per hour.

AMPHIBIOUS BOATS

The SEALs use a variety of small boats for their missions both on land and in water.

SMALL BOATS

One of the most useful SEAL boats is the Rigid Hull Inflatable Boat (RHIB). This boat is 36 feet (11 meters) long and can carry three crew members and eight SEALs. A fast boat, it can travel at 40 miles (64 kilometers) per hour over the water. It can also be armed with machine guns and other weapons. Another SEAL boat is the Special Operations Craft-Riverine (SOC-R). Another speedy craft, it is designed to operate in the shallow waters of rivers.

RUBBER DINGHY

The basic SEAL inflatable dinghy is the F470 Combat Rubber Raiding Craft (CRRC). It can be pushed forward with paddles, as we can see here, or it can be fitted with a motor for faster travel across the water.

BULLETPROOF

The F470 boat can be fitted with a special inflatable kit that makes the boat bulletproof.

PADDLING

Using paddles is still an important SEAL skill. Paddling is one of the quietest ways of getting ashore.

MARK V SOC

The boat seen here is the Mark V Special Operations Craft (SOC). The purpose of this boat is to drop off SEAL divers near enemy coastlines. It is also used to hunt down and stop smaller enemy boats. The Mark V can carry up to 16 fully equipped SEALs. It can also sail for more than 500 miles (805 kilometers) and at speeds of more than 40 miles (64 kilometers) per hour.

UNDERWATER VESSELS

The U.S. Navy SEALs have some incredible craft for moving people and equipment silently under water.

SEAL DELIVERY VEHICLE

The SEAL Delivery Vehicle (SDV) is basically a miniature submarine. It measures 22 feet (seven meters) in length. Inside, it holds a crew of two SEALs plus a SEAL Combat Swimmer team. The SEAL crew often take part in the mission as well. In the big picture here, the front end of an SDV is open, and a SEAL diving team is heading out on a training mission.

SUBMARINES

SDVs can sail off from the decks of specially adapted Navy submarines. SEAL divers are also trained to live and work aboard Navy submarines because the large submarines can sail thousands of miles (kilometers) to SEAL target areas.

SUBMERSIBLE

The SDV is properly known as a "submersible." The inside of the SDV is actually flooded with water, so the SEALs have to wear breathing gear at all times.

THE ASDS

The SEALs also had their own submarine called the Advanced SEAL Delivery System. It is no longer used.

AIRDROPPED

A large aircraft can also drop the SDV into the ocean for long-range missions.

AIRCRAFT

The SEALs are flown into action by the aircraft of the U.S. Navy, U.S. Army, and U.S. Air Force.

HELICOPTERS

Helicopters are the most useful aircraft to U.S. Navy SEALs. They can take SEAL combat teams into places that are hard to reach by airplane, truck, or car. SEAL units will often fly in Navy helicopters such as the HH-60H Seahawk, seen here in the main picture. As well as holding SEALs, the Seahawk can carry its own weapons. These include Hellfire missiles, used for destroying enemy tanks.

DRONES

SEAL teams make use of Unmanned Aerial Vehicles (UAVs), or "drones." These mini-aircraft (see below) do not have a pilot. They can spy on enemy forces with on-board cameras.

DRONE FLIGHT

Drones are controlled from the ground by someone with remote flying controls. Without a pilot, drones can fly for many hours.

HEAVY LIFT

If SEALs have to fly into action with vehicles or heavy equipment, they will use more powerful aircraft. Good examples of these aircraft are the C-130 Hercules and the CH-47 Chinook helicopter.

LOW LEVEL

When Special Operations Forces aircraft fly into enemy territory, they stay low to avoid being spotted by enemy radar systems.

FAST-ROPING

SEALs use the fast-roping technique. It involves sliding down a rope beneath a hovering helicopter.

As soon as a SEAL team lands from a helicopter, they take up positions to defend themselves from enemy attack.

SPECIAL OPS— RESTORE HOPE

On October 3–4, 1993, SEALs were involved in a huge battle in Mogadishu, Somalia.

BACKGROUND

Mogadishu is a city in the country of Somalia, in Africa. In early October 1993, a mixed force of U.S. Army Rangers, U.S. Navy SEALs, and other U.S. soldiers were sent into the city to capture the leaders of a group that had been terrorizing the local people.

SHOT DOWN

Two of the helicopters sent into Mogadishu were shot down, and the Americans had to mount a rescue mission.

GUNFIRE FIGHT

SEALs from DEVGRU and other U.S. troops fought a gun battle for hours in the streets of Mogadishu before they were rescued. Nineteen U.S. soldiers were killed in the battle, but about 500 enemy soldiers were killed.

MARINES

U.S. Marines (seen here) were used in operations in Somalia. Like the SEALs, the Marines are also part of the U.S. Navy.

SPECIAL OPS— AFGHANISTAN

Since 2001, the SEALs have fought many battles in Afghanistan.

TRAINING

SEALs have been used to train local soldiers of the Afghan National Army (ANA). They train the Afghan men in using weapons and in fighting techniques.

HUNTING THE ENEMY

An important role of the SEALs in Afghanistan has been to hunt down leaders of the "Taliban" enemy. First, the SEAL teams received information about where they could find the enemy. Then, they flew into the area using helicopters, and attempted to surprise the enemy forces. These missions often led to gun battles in which the enemy commanders were either killed or captured.

Here SEALs land from the back of a Chinook helicopter for a mission in Afghanistan.

SEAL BRAVERY

In June 2005, four SEALs were sent on a mission to watch enemy forces in the Pech area of Afghanistan. The enemy discovered them after the SEALs encountered some goat herders and let them go. A battle went on for hours, and the SEALs killed or wounded dozens of enemy soldiers. Three of the four SEALs were killed, however. The fourth SEAL survived after being rescued by a local Afghan family.

INTELLIGENCE

SEALs in Afghanistan are used to gather "intelligence." This information about the enemy could be useful to U.S. forces.

SPECIAL OPS— THE HUNT FOR BIN LADEN

Osama bin Laden was the man who planned the attacks on the United States on September 11, 2001.

TRACKING HIM DOWN

For many years, the United States tried to find Osama bin Laden. Eventually, U.S. forces tracked him down. He was hiding in a large building in Abbottabad in the country of Pakistan. On May 2, 2011, SEAL Team 6, or DEVGRU, was sent to capture or kill him. They flew into action using top-secret helicopters that landed them right next to bin Laden's building.

SEAL DOG

The SEAL operation included a dog named "Cairo." He was a breed of dog called a Belgian Malinois. He helped track down people in hiding.

LONG QUEST

The hunt for Osama bin Laden began back in 2001. He hid for 10 years. The Central Intelligence Agency tracked him down.

NIGHT OPERATION

The mission was carried out during the nighttime. During the landings, one helicopter crashed, but all the SEALs managed to go into action.

KILLING BIN LADEN

The SEAL team hunted through the building, shooting several other members of bin Laden's family. They used night-vision goggles to see in the dark. Eventually, they cornered bin Laden in a bedroom, and killed him.

With the mission complete, helicopters took the SEALs back to safety. No SEAL was wounded or killed.

It is possible to experience SEAL training before actually joining the SEALs.

CADETS

Many young people who want to join the SEALs start out by joining the U.S. Navy League Cadet Corps (NLCC) and the U.S. Naval Sea Cadet Corps (NSCC). The NLCC is for people aged 10–13, and the NSCC is for people aged 13–17. Both organizations give boys and girls the chance to experience Navy life and training.

SEAL FIT CAMP

Adults wanting to do SEAL training can attend SEAL Fit Camp. SEAL instructors run these physical fitness camps.

NAVY LIFE

The NLCC and NSCC offer many different types of training. Cadets can visit ships and sit inside Navy aircraft. They can learn to sail small boats and navigate on the land. They also gain first-aid training. The cadets will also get the chance to wear uniforms and can be promoted up through ranks.

WEB INFO

Even though the SEALs are a secretive organization, they have a website for information. This is: navyseals.com

CAUTION!

Do not attempt any of the extreme training techniques used by the real Navy SEALs. They are designed for adult bodies, and could injure you.

GLOSSARY

ANTITANK WEAPONS: Weapons that are designed to destroy tanks used by the enemy

CAMOUFLAGE: A material or pattern used to hide or disguise something

CENTRAL INTELLIGENCE AGENCY: An independent U.S. government agency that provides information to key U.S. leaders so they can make important, informed decisions

COMBAT DIVING: Swimming underwater with equipment, often for fighting with others

COVERT: Describes something that is kept secret from the enemy and from most other people

DEMOLITIONS: The act of destroying things, especially with explosives

DEVGRU: An abbreviation for the United States Naval Special Warfare Development Group, a SEAL team specializing in fighting terrorism and rescuing hostages

EXPLOSIVES: Substances that can be made to shatter violently or burst apart, especially in bombs

EXTRACTION: Methods of getting soldiers out from enemy territory and back to safety

HELL WEEK: A five-and-a-half day training session in BUD/S, in which the recruits will have almost no sleep and will exercise constantly

HOSTAGES: People captured and held by an enemy or terrorist force

HUMVEE: A large four-wheel vehicle used by the SEALs

MACHINE GUNS: Automatic weapons that can quickly fire bullets without stopping

PARACHUTING: Jumping from aircraft using a device of light fabric shaped like an umbrella that allows the jumper to land safely on the earth

SCUBA: Self-Contained Underwater Breathing Apparatus

SDVT: SEAL Delivery Vehicle Team, a special group of SEALs who are able to land SEAL units in enemy territory using boats and underwater craft

TACTICS: The methods that are used to beat the enemy in battle. Tactics are often the ways that military forces are arranged and moved

TALIBAN: A religious and political group that wants to enforce strict laws of the religion of Islam and supports using fear and violent crimes to achieve its goal

TELESCOPIC SIGHT: A piece of equipment used to see objects from faraway

TRIDENT: A spear with three points that stick out of it

VIET CONG: Communist forces from South Vietnam that were fighting their government, helped by soldiers from North Vietnam

SEALs must have complete confidence in their buddies, as they will have to fight side by side in battle.

INDEX